HEROES OF FAITH

DOUGLAS CONNELLY

8 STUDIES
FOR INDIVIDUALS
OR GROUPS

INTER-VARSITY PRESS
36 Causton Street, London SW1P 4ST, England
Email: ivp@ivpbooks.com
Website: www.ivpbooks.com

Originally published in the United States of America in the LifeGuide® Bible Studies series in 2011 by InterVarsity Press, Downers Grove, Illinois
First published in Great Britain by Scripture Union in 2012
This edition published in Great Britain by Inter-Varsity Press 2019

British Library Cataloguing-in-Publication Data
A catalogue record for this book is available from the British Library.

ISBN: 978–1–78359–833–5

Printed in Great Britain by Ashford Colour Press Ltd, Gosport, Hampshire

Inter-Varsity Press publishes Christian books that are true to the Bible and that communicate the gospel, develop discipleship and strengthen the church for its mission in the world.

IVP originated within the Inter-Varsity Fellowship, now the Universities and Colleges Christian Fellowship, a student movement connecting Christian Unions in universities and colleges throughout Great Britain, and a member movement of the International Fellowship of Evangelical Students. Website: www.uccf.org.uk. That historic association is maintained, and all senior IVP staff and committee members subscribe to the UCCF Basis of Faith.

Contents

Getting the Most Out of *Heroes of Faith*

We all need heroes. We respect and value the people who have set an example for our lives or who have pioneered the way in our careers or who have guided us through difficult times. The Bible has its heroes too—men and women who embody what it means to trust God and to follow his direction. The writer of Hebrews set up an entire gallery of spiritual portraits for us to remember and pattern our lives after. These are individuals who learned in tough times to stretch themselves out in faith on an almighty God and on his unfailing promises.

This study guide will introduce you not just to a series of Bible characters but also to a fascinating collection of role models who will help you forge your own heroic faith. Your relationships, your vision of the future, your walk with God will change forever as you discover the principles of courageous faith and as you implement those principles in your personal life and in the life of your church. The journey won't be easy. If you are cowardly or faint-hearted, turn back now! But at the end of this spiritual journey you will find a new kind of strength and purpose—the courage that comes from trust in a promise-keeping God.

Suggestions for Individual Study

1. As you begin each study, pray that God will speak to you through his Word.

2. Read the introduction to the study and respond to the personal reflection question or exercise. This is designed to help you focus on God and on the theme of the study.

3. Each study deals with a particular passage so that you can delve into the author's meaning in that context. Read and re-read the passage to be studied. The questions are written using the language of the New International Version, so you may wish to use that version of the Bible. The New Revised Standard Version is also recommended.

4. This is an inductive Bible study, designed to help you discover for yourself what Scripture is saying. The study includes three types of questions. *Observation* questions ask about the basic facts: who, what, when, where and how. *Interpretation* questions delve into the meaning of the passage. *Application* questions help you discover the implications of the text for growing in Christ. These three keys unlock the treasures of Scripture.

Write your answers to the questions in the spaces provided or in a personal journal. Writing can bring clarity and deeper understanding of yourself and of God's Word.

5. It might be good to have a Bible dictionary handy. Use it to look up any unfamiliar words, names or places.

6. Use the prayer suggestion to guide you in thanking God for what you have learned and to pray about the applications that have come to mind.

7. You may want to go on to the suggestion under "Now or Later," or you may want to use that idea for your next study.

Suggestions for Members of a Group Study

1. Come to the study prepared. Follow the suggestions for individual study mentioned above. You will find that careful preparation will greatly enrich your time spent in group discussion.

2. Be willing to participate in the discussion. The leader of your group will not be lecturing. Instead, he or she will be encouraging the members of the group to discuss what they have learned. The leader will be asking the questions that are found in this guide.

3. Stick to the topic being discussed. Your answers should be based on the verses which are the focus of the discussion and not on outside authorities such as commentaries or speakers. These studies focus on a particular passage of Scripture. Only rarely should you refer to other portions of the Bible. This allows for everyone to participate in in-depth study on equal ground.

4. Be sensitive to the other members of the group. Listen attentively when they describe what they have learned. You may be surprised by their insights! Each question assumes a variety of answers. Many questions do not have "right" answers, particularly questions that aim at meaning or application. Instead the questions push us to explore the passage more thoroughly.

When possible, link what you say to the comments of others. Also, be affirming whenever you can. This will encourage some of the more hesitant members of the group to participate.

5. Be careful not to dominate the discussion. We are sometimes so eager to express our thoughts that we leave too little opportunity for others to respond. By all means participate! But allow others to also.

6. Expect God to teach you through the passage being discussed and through the other members of the group. Pray that you will have an enjoyable and profitable time together, but also that as a result of the study you will find ways that you can take action individually and/or as a group.

7. Remember that anything said in the group is considered confidential and should not be discussed outside the group unless specific permission is given to do so.

8. If you are the group leader, you will find additional suggestions at the back of the guide.

1

Pleasing God

Abel

**Hebrews 11:1-6;
Genesis 4:1-12**

The little girl stood on the edge of the playscape looking down at her father, who was standing with his arms held out. "Jump," he said. "You know I'll catch you."

For just a moment indecision crossed her sweet face. She glanced back at the ramp she had just walked up to get to this level and briefly considered walking back down to the ground. But then a wide smile broke across her face as she looked back at her daddy—and with a squeal of delight she leaped into the air.

GROUP DISCUSSION. Tell the group about a time when you had to trust another person for safety or rescue. Were you "caught" (like the girl in her father's arms), or did you come away disappointed?

PERSONAL REFLECTION. In what circumstances do you find it most difficult to trust someone else? How do you respond to that sense of mistrust?

The author of the book of Hebrews wants to challenge us to a life of active faith in our faithful God. He closes chapter 10 by pointing out that we are not among those who shrink back from a courageous commitment to Christ but instead are "of those who believe and are saved" (10:39). We have personal confidence in Jesus' sacrifice on the cross to make us right with God. Then, in chapter 11, the writer encourages us to live out that faith in the decisions and experiences of life. This kind of living faith springs from our will—our willingness to trust God even when we cannot see what the future holds. *Read Hebrews 11:1-6.*

---

1. Though we don't know for sure who wrote the book of Hebrews, what observations can you make about the author based on these opening verses of chapter 11?

---

2. What words stand out to you in the description of faith in verse 1? Explain why each is significant to you.

What words would you use to describe the level of faith in your life right now?

---

3. What are the things you hope for as a follower of Christ?

4. What does faith help us grasp about the universe around us (v. 3)?

Read Genesis 4:1-12.

---

5. What do you learn about God's character from this account?

---

6. What do Cain's responses both to God's rejection of his offering (v. 5) and to God's warning (vv. 6-7) reveal about this man?

---

7. Hebrews 11:4 says that "by faith Abel offered God a better sacrifice." How was his sacrifice better than Cain's?

In what sense does Abel still speak to us?

---

8. Verse 6 of Hebrews 11 sets the tone for every example of faith that we will explore in this passage. Why does faith please God?

9. In what area of your life is it easy for you to take on Cain's attitude toward God or others?

What practices could help you walk in Abel's way to please God in your life?

Ask God to give you the kind of faith that produces faithful obedience to him.

Now or Later

Verse 5 of Hebrews 11 addresses one more "hero of faith": Enoch. His life is summed up in just four verses in the Old Testament (Genesis 5:21-24)—fifty-one words in the New International Version! Yet the author of Hebrews singles him out as a man of great faith. What marked Enoch out was that he "walked with God" (Genesis 5:24) and he "pleased God" (Hebrews 11:5). Enoch's relationship with God was so close that his removal from earth to heaven didn't interrupt a thing! What would you ask Enoch if you could interview him today? What desires does Enoch's walk of faith prompt in you?

2

Making Difficult Choices

Noah

Hebrews 11:7;
Genesis 6:5-22

Catastrophe movies are big business. Oceans rise to swallow cities, pandemics wipe out nations, alien spaceships blast bridges and skyscrapers. We sit in our seats surrounded by images of destruction and disaster—and then walk out to the lobby to get a refill on our popcorn! While we're stunned by the visual effects on the screen, we also realize that what we're seeing isn't really happening.

GROUP DISCUSSION. What catastrophes do you think could happen in the next ten years? What can you do to be prepared?

PERSONAL REFLECTION. Are you someone who tries to prepare for every possible situation, or are you more willing just to take things as they come? What is the downside of your particular approach to the unexpected events of life?

The Bible has its own share of catastrophes—real ones. A massive flood, for example, destroyed every human being on earth except for Noah and his family, floating on the surface of the turbulent water in a crude barge. All Noah had to rely on as he did the tedious, laborious work of building the ark was God's warning of a disaster yet to come. Clearly, his choice to believe God was not an easy one to make. *Read Hebrews 11:7 and Genesis 6:5-22.*

---

1. What "things not yet seen" did God tell Noah about (Hebrews 11:7)?

---

2. Why did God choose Noah and his family to be the survivors (Genesis 6:8-9)?

Those who believe in Jesus as Lord and Savior are also "survivors," like Noah and his family. Why has God chosen to rescue us?

---

3. In what tangible ways did Noah express his trust in what God had told him?

4. What does Noah's example tell us about the relationship between confident trust in God and the hard work of preparation?

What is the danger of imbalance on either side?

5. Do you think the fact that Noah actually heard God's voice helped him obey God in building the ark? Explain why or why not.

6. Describe the condition of human society just before the flood (Genesis 6:5, 11-12).

7. What would you have found most difficult about raising three sons to maturity in a culture like that?

8. It may have taken Noah 120 years to build the ark and yet, in all that time, it seems that only his own family believed his witness. What do these "results" tell you about God's expectations of us as his followers?

9. The apostle Peter called Noah "a preacher of righteousness" (2 Peter 2:5). The author of Hebrews says that by faith Noah condemned the world. What warning from God do you think should be raised in our society?

10. What is something difficult God is asking you to do?

How does Noah's example encourage you?

Pray about your own willingness to stand true to God in a world that is drifting away from him. Ask for "holy fear" to obey his Word.

Now or Later

Find a quiet, solitary place and sit in silence before the Lord. Listen as you ask God one question: "Where is one place in my life where I need to step out in faith?" Write down what you hear in your spirit from the Lord. Share it with a trusted friend. Then, in serious respect for God, do it!

3

Believing the Impossible

Abraham and Sarah

Hebrews 11:8-16;
Genesis 18:1-15; 21:1-7

When I think of a person of faith, I think of George Strickland. He was the spiritual "patriarch" of a church I pastored for more than ten years. When the congregation had grown well beyond the capacity of our facilities, we met to decide if we should take up the challenge of moving to a new location. After all the debate had gone back and forth, Mr. Strickland stood and urged us to step out in confident faith. "This church was born as an act of faith in God's ability to do great things," he said. "We cannot hesitate to trust him now." His passionate appeal settled the issue.

GROUP DISCUSSION. Who in your life do you think of as a person of faith and why?

PERSONAL REFLECTION. Do you think your family or friends consider you to be a person of faith? Why or why not?

When the writers of Scripture wanted a model of faith, their eyes almost always turned to Abraham. Other men and women lived lives of impressive faith, but no one's faith is celebrated like Abraham's. *Read Hebrews 11:8-16 and Genesis 18:1-15; 21:1-7.*

1. According to Hebrews 11:8-16, in what situations did Abraham exhibit faith?

2. What price did Abraham pay to respond obediently to God's call?

3. When has God called you to leave behind what you're comfortable with to take a similar step of faith?

4. While in Canaan, Abraham and Sarah were visited by three strangers. Hospitality to strangers was a social obligation in the ancient Middle East. Do you think Abraham sensed something special about these three men by the way he treated them (Genesis 18:1-8)? Explain.

5. The Lord made a promise to Abraham and Sarah when he

visited them (Genesis 18:10). Why did his promise cause Sarah to laugh and require such great faith for both Abraham and Sarah (Genesis 18:10-12; Hebrews 11:11-12)?

---

6. About what situation or circumstance is God telling you that it is never too late?

What can you believe God to do in that seemingly impossible situation, based on the way God kept his promises to Abraham (Hebrews 11:12)?

---

7. Why does the writer of Hebrews hold Abraham and Sarah up (with others) as examples of those who finish life well (Hebrews 11:13)?

---

8. What "city" was Abraham seeking (Hebrews 11:10)?

Why was that a mark of faith?

9. God called Abraham to follow him to a new land, but what was the real pilgrimage God called him to?

10. What can you learn from Hebrews 11:14-16 about the focus of your own spiritual pilgrimage?

11. How does God respond to those who diligently seek after him (Hebrews 11:16)?

Think quietly about the fact that God is not ashamed to be your God. Recommit yourself to seeking after him in your daily journey.

Now or Later

As you reflect on a situation or relationship in your life that seems "as good as dead" (see question six in the study), write down some of the reasons it is hard for you to trust God for that need. How are you responding to the long wait for God to intervene? Consider what steps you can take to increase your faith in this difficult time of waiting. Pray through those steps and ask God to help you cultivate a deeper trust in him and in his faithfulness.

4

Anticipating God's Blessing

Isaac

Hebrews 11:17-20;
Genesis 27:1-40

Our kids pick up a lot from us. Sometimes that makes us proud—like when they imitate our perseverance and get all A's on their report card or when they inherit our work ethic and athleticism and kick the winning goal in soccer. At other times we are a little embarrassed by our influence—like when my son shouted at another driver from his car seat in the back: "Watch out, you idiot!" Where did he learn that? Our children often become very much like us—for good or not so good.

GROUP DISCUSSION. Tell the group a story about a time when you caught yourself acting or talking like one of your parents.

PERSONAL REFLECTION. What good traits in your life would you trace to the influence of your parents? What areas of struggle can you link to their example?

Isaac lived in the shadow of his famous father, Abraham. His birth was the beginning of the fulfillment of God's promises to Abraham, but Isaac seems to fade into the background in the presence of his faith-filled father. The truth, though, is that Isaac was a man of faith too, as the writer of Hebrews reminds us. *Read Hebrews 11:17-20.*

1. What do we learn about Isaac in these verses?

2. Isaac's name first appears in Hebrews 11 in the context of God's command to Abraham to sacrifice him. What do you think Isaac would have remembered most from this experience of sacrifice and rescue as he grew into adulthood?

How do you think those memories would have affected his relationship with God?

Read Genesis 27:1-40.

3. In time, Isaac had sons of his own, Jacob and Esau. How would you describe these twin brothers based on Genesis 27?

4. In the culture of Isaac's day, the father's blessing—a promise of prosperity and the inheritance of prominence over the family—was given to the firstborn son. Yet in Genesis 25:23, when Isaac's wife, Rebekah, became pregnant with Esau and Jacob, God told her that "the older [son] will serve the younger." Why do you think Isaac still planned to give Esau his blessing?

_____

5. What does Jacob and Rebekah's deception reveal about their relationship with and trust in God for the future?

Where is your level of trust in God for the future compared to theirs?

_____

6. Does Jacob's success in deceiving Isaac demonstrate God's approval of his actions? Why or why not?

_____

7. The author of Hebrews says that Isaac acted "by faith" when he blessed Jacob and Esau in regard to their future (11:20). How was Isaac's response to this deception an act of faith?

8. Whose blessing or approval means the most to you and why?

9. Where have you seen God's blessing and grace in your own life?

Where are you experiencing great disappointment?

10. What can you learn from this account that will increase your level of active faith in God?

Ask God to help you trust him fully for your future, and for the futures of those you love.

Now or Later

Think about the relationships within your own family. Are there deceptions and wounds that you have been responsible for? Have you been the wounded one? How can you begin the process of healing? Determine to take one step toward reconciliation or restoration this week as an act of faith in God's power and grace.

5

Faith for
the Future

Jacob

**Hebrews 11:20-22;
Genesis 48:1-22**

It's never easy to see a person we love come to the end of life.
Sometimes that person is taken suddenly, and we live with re-
grets about things we should have said. At other times the person knows death is coming and therefore has the opportunity
to express their love and comfort to those left behind. Those
"final words" have the potential to inspire and guide an entire
generation.

GROUP DISCUSSION. Talk about someone who has left a legacy in
your life. Does their influence move you to greater achievement
in life, or is it a source of woundedness? What would you say to
that person today?

PERSONAL REFLECTION. What spiritual legacy are you leaving?
How can you communicate your blessing to your children,
family or friends?

The legacy of faith that started with Abraham powerfully guided and influenced the generations after him—starting with his son Isaac and then flowing down to Isaac's son Jacob. They too learned to trust God even when it seemed that God's promises had failed. Now, as Jacob draws near to death, he demonstrates the faith of his ancestors by passing on the blessing of God's promises to his sons and grandsons, particularly the two sons of his son Joseph. *Read Hebrews 11:20-22 and Genesis 48:1-22.*

---

1. According to Hebrews 11, how did each of Abraham's descendants—Isaac, Jacob and Joseph—demonstrate faith in God's promises to give them a land to dwell in and to make them a great people?

---

2. What promise from God about the future do you hold to most passionately?

How does that confidence in the future affect the way you live today?

---

3. Jacob was the most deceitful and scheming of Abraham's descendants and yet, at the end of his life, he demonstrated remarkable trust in God's ability to keep his promises. What factors might have brought Jacob from the place of a schemer to the place of such confidence in God's plan (see Genesis 48:3-11, 15-16)?

4. Why is it significant that Jacob claimed Ephraim and Manasseh as his own sons (Genesis 48:5-6)?

5. What did Jacob do toward Joseph's sons that was unexpected—and why was Joseph upset about it (Genesis 48:13-14, 17-19)?

6. What was God demonstrating by having Jacob switch hands for the blessing?

What does this event say to you about how God may choose to bring blessing into your life as you seek to follow him?

7. Jacob blessed Joseph's sons in the name of God (Genesis 48:15-16, 20). How would it make you feel to have a parent or a spiritually mature friend make such an evaluation and prophecy about you and your future?

8. How did Jacob's words to Joseph express Jacob's faith in the future (Genesis 48:21-22)?

9. Out of Jacob's entire life of 147 years, the writer of Hebrews singles out this act of blessing Joseph's sons as the outstanding example of Jacob's faith. If Hebrews 11 were still being written, what act of confidence in God would stand out as the demonstration of your faith?

10. The writer of Hebrews also sees Jacob's blessing on Joseph's sons as an act of worship (11:21). How is confidence in God's promises for the future an act of worship?

11. As an act of worship and faith, what spiritual strengths would you like to pass on to your children or to others upon whom you have some influence?

Ask the Holy Spirit to give you insight into the future spiritual development of those you influence and love. Seek to give them wise direction.

Now or Later

As Jacob blesses Joseph and his sons, he recalls how God has been his shepherd and his guardian angel (Genesis 48:15-16). Think of ways that God has been a shepherd to you to guide you and provide for you, or how God has been an angel to protect you from harm. Speak your own words of thanks or praise to God for his involvement and intervention in your life. Share one of your God-encounter experiences with a friend this week.

6

Resting on a Trustworthy God

Moses

Hebrews 11:23-29;
Exodus 12:21-36

The young woman's voice shook with emotion as she spoke at her grandmother's funeral. "No matter what I was going through," she said, "I knew my grandmother was praying for me every day. But now I wonder who will take her place? Who will be as faithful to pray? Who will be my example of such trust in God?"

GROUP DISCUSSION. What has been the hardest or most challenging experience of your life? Who helped you through it?

PERSONAL REFLECTION. Who has been the most significant "nurturer" in your life in the ways of the Lord? How has that person influenced your personal development? How have you communicated your gratitude for their godly influence?

Moses, the next hero in the gallery of faith in Hebrews 11, was an example of faith to the Israelites. God used him to deliver the people of Israel from the oppression of slavery, and that work of liberation was an act of faith from beginning to end. Several times the writer of Hebrews uses the familiar words "by faith" to describe Moses' journey with the Lord. At each crucial step in the deliverance of his people, Moses put his trust in the God who will not fail. *Read Hebrews 11:23-29.*

---

1. What aspects of Moses' story are you most familiar with?

Is there anything in this passage that is new or surprising to you? Explain.

---

2. The initial step of faith did not come from Moses but from his parents (v. 23). Even though Scripture doesn't give us many clues, what factors can you think of that may have made them recognize that Moses was not an ordinary child?

---

3. The second stage of Moses' faith journey involved identifying himself with his own people. There were two decisions involved in that identification (vv. 24-26). Explain the two decisions and the consequences of each.

4. What signs of success in our culture might God ask you to turn from as an expression of your confident trust in him?

5. What reward was Moses looking forward to?

6. Moses spent forty years in the wilderness of Midian, waiting for God's deliverance of the Israelites. How can we, like Moses, keep our eyes on God as we wait for his fulfillment of his promises?

Read Exodus 12:21-36.

7. What aspects of God's character are revealed in the account of the Passover?

8. Do you find it difficult to trust in a God who deals so severely with those who oppose him? Why or why not?

9. Why did it require faith for Moses and the Israelites to follow God's instructions about the lamb and the blood?

10. The final step of faith for Moses highlighted in Hebrews 11 is the crossing of the Red Sea (found in Exodus 14). How was that an act of faith for both Moses and the Israelites as a whole?

---

11. Have you seen one person's faith influence a larger group today, the way Moses' did? If so, explain.

---

12. What situation is your personal "Egypt," where you need to trust God for deliverance?

Ask God to set you free from any spiritual bondage or oppression. Seek to live a life marked by faith wherever you are in the process of deliverance—stuck, leaving, waiting, set free.

Now or Later

Moses' life fell into three forty-year periods: the time in Egypt when he was being raised, apart from God, as the son of Pharoah's daughter; the time in Midian when he questioned God's call; and the time in the wilderness when he led God's people. Decide which of those phases you are in right now. What can you do to demonstrate confidence in God where you are today? Ask a trusted friend to help you evaluate your life's journey so far—and to hold you accountable to keep moving forward in a walk of faithfulness.

7

Facing Our Fears

Rahab

**Hebrews 11:30-31;
Joshua 2:1-21**

In college I led a Bible study that started as a small group but then grew until anywhere from thirty to fifty students would come each week, crowding into a classroom where we'd pray and study God's Word. There was one student on campus, however, who ridiculed, intimidated and mocked anyone who was or wanted to be part of the group. One day I had heard enough from him and blurted out, "Why don't you just come one time and see what it's all about?" I couldn't believe his response. He said, "No one's ever asked me to come." So the next week he attended—and the week after that. In time the critic believed in Jesus and began to invite other students to come. The least likely person became an ardent follower of Christ.

GROUP DISCUSSION. What person or kind of person would you feel most uncomfortable talking to about Jesus? Be honest about your fears.

PERSONAL REFLECTION. When do you find your commitment to Jesus to be most embarrassing or unnerving? Think about a situation you have faced when you were reluctant to share or were silent about your faith.

Rahab, the last person the author of Hebrews talks about in any detail in his gallery of faith heroes, is the one who seems least likely to be included in the list. For one thing, she was a woman. In the Jewish culture from which the book of Hebrews emerges, men were usually picked first as models of holy living. Moreover, Rahab was a non-Jew (a Gentile). Why would a Jewish teacher writing to a Jewish audience pick a non-Jewish woman as an example of fearless faith? But the main reason she seems least likely to appear in Hebrews 11 is that she was a prostitute. Some biblical scholars have tried to get around that moral issue, but the language of Scripture is clear. What's also clear from Scripture, though, is that Rahab demonstrated outstanding trust in God in a remarkable act of courage. *Read Hebrews 11:30-31 and Joshua 2:1-21.*

---

1. What character traits of Rahab emerge from this encounter in Joshua 2?

---

2. The unbelieving Israelite generation that had left Egypt had all died in the wilderness. Now the new generation was ready to enter the land God had promised long before to Abraham, which is why Joshua, Israel's new leader, sent the two spies into the land. Why do you think the two spies went to a prostitute's house?

3. Rahab's first work of faith was a lie! Was Rahab right or wrong to lie about the presence of the spies (Joshua 2:4-6)? Explain your answer.

How would you have handled the dilemma?

4. What did Rahab want from the spies in exchange for concealing them on the roof (Joshua 2:12-13)?

5. If Rahab was simply bargaining for her safety, why does the writer see Rahab's willingness to welcome and hide the spies as an act of extraordinary faith (Hebrews 11:31)?

6. What acts of faith were required of Rahab after the spies left the city (Joshua 2:17-20)?

7. Explain what Rahab's obedience reveals about her relationship to the Lord God.

8. Rahab's action led to her family's deliverance. What steps can you take that might lead to the spiritual deliverance of your family or circle of friends?

9. Rahab's story reminds us that no one—not even our enemy, as Rahab initially was to the Israelites—is beyond God's reach. What groups or individuals in your circle of acquaintances—or outside—have you written off as unreachable?

10. What can you do this week as an act of faith to begin to reach one of those people?

Commit your fears to the Lord and trust him to give you the courage to act in faith.

Now or Later

Rahab is mentioned two other times in the New Testament. James points to her as a model of believers who demonstrate true faith by their works, even declaring that she was "considered righteous for what she did" (James 2:25). The other reference is in the genealogy of Jesus in Matthew 1:5. One of Jesus' ancestors, a man named Salmon, married Rahab, the former prostitute. What does that fact tell you about God's grace? What hope does it bring to you about how God can work through you? When you see a prostitute or someone else on the margins of society, will you write them off as unreachable, or will you think of Rahab?

8

Your Heroic Faith

Hebrews 11:32–12:3

As a young pastor I was waiting to have prayer with some of the church leaders one Sunday morning before the worship service when an usher came into my office with an announcement. "Two of your seminary professors and their wives are here," he crowed. "They've come to hear you preach!"

A knot formed in my stomach as I looked out and saw not only one of my theology teachers but also the man who taught young seminarians to preach. I flashed through my sermon in my mind, hoping that I at least came close to the model of biblical exposition he had taught us. The presence of these highly respected "witnesses" made my knees shake a little.

But their presence also gave me a jolt of empowerment and confidence. God had called me to a task and these men had helped prepare me. Their presence inspired me to embrace the challenge that was before me.

GROUP DISCUSSION. Who is your "hero" in business or sports or entertainment? How would you feel, for example, if your golf hero showed up just as you were about to tee off, or your favorite musical artist came to hear you sing a solo at church?

PERSONAL REFLECTION. In whose presence do you feel most scrutinized or judged? In whose presence do you feel most encouraged and challenged? Which way do you feel in God's presence?

The writer of Hebrews concludes his challenge to live a life of confident trust in God by moving away from individuals and embracing the whole company of men and women who down through the centuries had determined to live by faith. These faithful believers—some named, most unnamed—become a great host of witnesses prompting us to follow in their path. This great passage on faith that we've been studying ends with a call to all of us today who want our lives to be marked by courageous faith. *Read Hebrews 11:32–12:3.*

---

1. What outcome to faith ties the first group of people together (vv. 32-35a)?

---

2. What is your response when you hear or read about a Christian who has experienced some remarkable work of God? Joy? Envy? Awe? Something else? Explain.

---

3. What is the outcome to faith for those in the second group listed in this passage (vv. 35b-38)?

Why do you think the writer includes them?

---

4. Both those who saw God's miraculous deliverance and those who died without seeing it were "commended for their faith" (v. 39). What does this say about claims today that genuine faith will always bring deliverance or prosperity or healing?

---

5. The author of Hebrews sees the men and women of faith who lived in the past to be "a great cloud of witnesses" (12:1). What does that mean to you as you pursue a deeper level of confident trust in God in your own life?

---

6. The life of faith is compared in Hebrews 12:1-3 to a race. Explain each of these elements as they apply to an actual race and as they apply to the pursuit of faithfulness in your life.

   a. "Throw off everything that hinders"

   b. "The sin that so easily entangles"

   c. "Run with perseverance"

   d. "The race marked out for us"

7. Of what value is it to keep our eyes fixed on Jesus in the race of faith (12:2)?

———————————————————

8. Jesus endured the cross and the opposition of sinful people. What should the example of Jesus' endurance produce in our lives (12:2-3)?

———————————————————

9. Where would you place yourself right now in the race toward a faith-filled life: on the bench? running steadily? ready to quit? sidetracked by a different goal? Explain.

What steps do these verses suggest you can take to get back in the race (or stay in it, if that is the case for you) for the long haul?

Focus your heart in renewed allegiance to Jesus alone. Ask God to help you get back or remain in the race—and to persevere to the end.

Now or Later

As you think back through the men and women of faith that we have studied, which one do you have the most in common with? Which situation would you find most difficult?

Leader's Notes

MY GRACE IS SUFFICIENT FOR YOU. (2 COR 12:9)

Leading a Bible discussion can be an enjoyable and rewarding experience. But it can also be *scary*—especially if you've never done it before. If this is your feeling, you're in good company. When God asked Moses to lead the Israelites out of Egypt, he replied, "O Lord, please send someone else to do it!" (Ex 4:13). It was the same with Solomon, Jeremiah and Timothy, but God helped these people in spite of their weaknesses, and he will help you as well.

You don't need to be an expert on the Bible or a trained teacher to lead a Bible discussion. The idea behind these inductive studies is that the leader guides group members to discover for themselves what the Bible has to say. This method of learning will allow group members to remember much more of what is said than a lecture would.

These studies are designed to be led easily. As a matter of fact, the flow of questions through the passage from observation to interpretation to application is so natural that you may feel that the studies lead themselves. This study guide is also flexible. You can use it with a variety of groups—student, professional, neighborhood or church groups. Each study takes forty-five to sixty minutes in a group setting.

There are some important facts to know about group dynamics and encouraging discussion. The suggestions listed below should enable you to effectively and enjoyably fulfill your role as leader.

Preparing for the Study

1. Ask God to help you understand and apply the passage in your own life. Unless this happens, you will not be prepared to lead others. Pray too for the various members of the group. Ask God to open your hearts to the message of his Word and motivate you to action.

2. Read the introduction to the entire guide to get an overview of the

entire book and the issues which will be explored.

3. As you begin each study, read and reread the assigned Bible passage to familiarize yourself with it.

4. This study guide is based on the New International Version of the Bible. It will help you and the group if you use this translation as the basis for your study and discussion.

5. Carefully work through each question in the study. Spend time in meditation and reflection as you consider how to respond.

6. Write your thoughts and responses in the space provided in the study guide. This will help you to express your understanding of the passage clearly.

7. It might help to have a Bible dictionary handy. Use it to look up any unfamiliar words, names or places. (For additional help on how to study a passage, see chapter five of *How to Lead a LifeBuilder Study*, IVP, 2018.)

8. Consider how you can apply the Scripture to your life. Remember that the group will follow your lead in responding to the studies. They will not go any deeper than you do.

9. Once you have finished your own study of the passage, familiarize yourself with the leader's notes for the study you are leading. These are designed to help you in several ways. First, they tell you the purpose the study guide author had in mind when writing the study. Take time to think through how the study questions work together to accomplish that purpose. Second, the notes provide you with additional background information or suggestions on group dynamics for various questions. This information can be useful when people have difficulty understanding or answering a question. Third, the leader's notes can alert you to potential problems you may encounter during the study.

10. If you wish to remind yourself of anything mentioned in the leader's notes, make a note to yourself below that question in the study.

Leading the Study

1. Begin the study on time. Open with prayer, asking God to help the group to understand and apply the passage.

2. Be sure that everyone in your group has a study guide. Encourage the group to prepare beforehand for each discussion by reading the introduction to the guide and by working through the questions in the study.

3. At the beginning of your first time together, explain that these studies are meant to be discussions, not lectures. Encourage the members of the group to participate. However, do not put pressure on those who may be hesitant to speak during the first few sessions. You may want to suggest the following guidelines to your group.

☐ Stick to the topic being discussed.

☐ Your responses should be based on the verses which are the focus of the discussion and not on outside authorities such as commentaries or speakers.

☐ These studies focus on a particular passage of Scripture. Only rarely should you refer to other portions of the Bible. This allows for everyone to participate in in-depth study on equal ground.

☐ Anything said in the group is considered confidential and will not be discussed outside the group unless specific permission is given to do so.

☐ We will listen attentively to each other and provide time for each person present to talk.

☐ We will pray for each other.

4. Have a group member read the introduction at the beginning of the discussion.

5. Every session begins with a group discussion question. The question or activity is meant to be used before the passage is read. The question introduces the theme of the study and encourages group members to begin to open up. Encourage as many members as possible to participate, and be ready to get the discussion going with your own response.

This section is designed to reveal where our thoughts or feelings need to be transformed by Scripture. That is why it is especially important not to read the passage before the discussion question is asked. The passage will tend to color the honest reactions people would otherwise give because they are, of course, supposed to think the way the Bible does.

You may want to supplement the group discussion question with an ice-breaker to help people to get comfortable. See the community section of the *Small Group Starter Kit* (IVP, 1995) for more ideas.

You also might want to use the personal reflection question with your group. Either allow a time of silence for people to respond individually or discuss it together.

6. Have a group member (or members if the passage is long) read aloud the passage to be studied. Then give people several minutes to read the passage again silently so that they can take it all in.

7. Question 1 will generally be an overview question designed to briefly survey the passage. Encourage the group to look at the whole passage, but try to avoid getting sidetracked by questions or issues that will be addressed later in the study.

8. As you ask the questions, keep in mind that they are designed to be used just as they are written. You may simply read them aloud. or you may prefer to express them in your own words.

There may be times when it is appropriate to deviate from the study guide. For example, a question may have already been answered. If so, move on to the next question. Or someone may raise an important question not covered in the guide. Take time to discuss it, but try to keep the group from going off on tangents.

9. Avoid answering your own questions. If necessary, repeat or rephrase them until they are clearly understood. Or point out something you read in the leader's notes to clarify the context or meaning. An eager group quickly becomes passive and silent if they think the leader will do most of the talking.

10. Don't be afraid of silence. People may need time to think about the question before formulating their answers.

11. Don't be content with just one answer. Ask, "What do the rest of you think?" or "Anything else?" until several people have given answers to the question.

12. Acknowledge all contributions. Try to be affirming whenever possible. Never reject an answer. If it is clearly off-base, ask, "Which verse led you to that conclusion?" or again, "What do the rest of you think?"

13. Don't expect every answer to be addressed to you, even though this will probably happen at first. As group members become more at ease, they will begin to truly interact with each other. This is one sign of healthy discussion.

14. Don't be afraid of controversy. It can be very stimulating. If you don't resolve an issue completely, don't be frustrated. Move on and keep it in mind for later. A subsequent study may solve the problem.

15. Periodically summarize what the group has said about the passage. This helps to draw together the various ideas mentioned and gives continuity to the study. But don't preach.

16. At the end of the Bible discussion you may want to allow group members a time of quiet to work on an idea under "Now or Later." Then discuss what you experienced. Or you may want to encourage group members to work on these ideas between meetings. Give an opportunity during the session for people to talk about what they are learning.

17. Conclude your time together with conversational prayer, adapting the prayer suggestion at the end of the study to your group. Ask for God's help in following through on the commitments you've made.

18. End on time.

Many more suggestions and helps are found in *How to Lead a LifeBuilder Study*.

Components of Small Groups
A healthy small group should do more than study the Bible. There are four components to consider as you structure your time together.

Nurture. Small groups help us to grow in our knowledge and love of God. Bible study is the key to making this happen and is the foundation of your small group.

Community. Small groups are a great place to develop deep friendships with other Christians. Allow time for informal interaction before and after each study. Plan activities and games that will help you get to know each other. Spend time having fun together going on a picnic or cooking dinner together.

Worship and prayer. Your study will be enhanced by spending time praising God together in prayer or song. Pray for each other's needs and keep track of how God is answering prayer in your group. Ask God to help you to apply what you are learning in your study.

Outreach. Reaching out to others can be a practical way of applying what you are learning, and it will keep your group from becoming self-focused. Host a series of evangelistic discussions for your friends or neighbors. Clean up the yard of an elderly friend. Serve at a soup kitchen together, or spend a day working in the community.

Many more suggestions and helps in each of these areas are found in the *Small Group Starter Kit*. You will also find information on building a small group. Reading through the starter kit will be worth your time.

Study 1.
Pleasing God: Abel.
Hebrews 11:1-6; Genesis 4:1-12.
Purpose: To introduce the challenges and blessings of a life marked by confident trust in God.
Question 1. The author of Hebrews was obviously a person who knew the Old Testament Scriptures well and who had a passion for cultivating a deep sense of trust in God in the readers of this letter. He (or she) also seems to be a person who had to exercise faith during his or her own difficult circumstances and saw God demonstrate himself to be absolutely faithful—"faith is being sure of what we hope for." In addition, the writer of Hebrews must have thought deeply about how the heroes of the Old Testament had

demonstrated faith in the experiences of life and what the implications of their faith-filled lives are for our lives as followers of Christ.

Question 2. This question is designed to get group members to think about how faith functions in the life of a Christian. Verse 1 of Hebrews 11 is not a definition of faith as much as it is a description of what faith produces. Confident trust in God produces certainty in our minds about what God will do in our lives. That assurance becomes convincing evidence of things we can't see yet but are confident will happen. This assurance that comes from faith allows the Christian to endure through times of difficulty or suffering.

As members of the group share their own perceptions of the level of faith in their lives, let them speak without judgment or comment from others. We may perceive someone as a person of strong faith, but they may see themselves in a very different light.

Question 3. Be prepared for a wide variety of answers to this question. A good follow-up question to each response is: What promise of God do you base your hope on? If a person has the confident hope that they will be with Christ after death, they have many promises from Scripture to rest that hope on. If, however, a person thinks that as a follower of Christ, they will become wealthy or never suffer, they'll have a much harder time finding biblical support for their hope.

Question 4. This question is not meant to open up a big debate in the group about creationism, intelligent design or God-guided evolution. The writer's point is that the confidence we have that God is the Creator stems from faith. We believe what God has said about himself and about how the universe came into existence, even though we may have differing opinions on the exact process God used. The writer of Hebrews makes an emphatic point that God created the visible universe out of nothing. God did not use preexisting material. it was God's will and God's power that formed all we see.

Question 5. The author of Hebrews assumes that his readers will be thoroughly acquainted with the Old Testament account of each of the models of faith he selects. You as the leader may need to do some extensive background reading so you can fill in the gaps in the group's knowledge. The story of Cain and Abel is fairly self-contained in Genesis 4. You may want to read the entire chapter yourself so you get the whole story.

We learn from this passage that God comes to each of us with grace. Even when God rejected Cain's offering and saw Cain's anger, he told Cain that if he did what was right (and did it with a submissive spirit) he would be accepted (4:6). The passage also reveals that God holds us accountable for our actions. Cain's actions were met with God's judgment.

Question 6. Cain's unwillingness to submit humbly to God is revealed in his response first to God's rejection of his offering and then to God's warning about allowing sinful impulses to control his behavior. Cain wanted his own way. Instead of responding in humble repentance, Cain chose the path of anger, rebellion and violence.

Question 7. As far as we can tell, the attitude of the worshiper was what entered into God's acceptance or rejection of these sacrifices. Abel offered his sacrifice by faith—with a heart of gratitude and trust in God. Cain offered his sacrifice in pride—reflected in his angry response to God when his offering was rejected. Some commentators have also concluded (based on the structure of the Hebrews text) that Abel went out of his way to bring the best offering to the Lord but that Cain simply discharged a duty (Allen Ross, *Creation and Blessing: A Guide to the Study and Exposition of Genesis* [Grand Rapids: Baker, 1988], p. 157). Certainly Cain's evil heart, seen only by God at first, revealed itself quickly in his resentment toward God and in the murder of his brother, in his uncooperative answers to God, and in his objection to God's punishment of him for his actions. The apostle John confirms Cain's evil actions and Abel's righteous ones in 1 John 3:11-12.

The story of Abel's faith still speaks generation after generation. We are still discussing it and puzzling over it thousands of years later! But the writer's statement also indicates that, from the very beginning of human history, men and women were made right with God on the basis of faith, not works. Abel was not righteous because he brought the best offering, but because he came with a heart of faith. It was his trust in God and his love for God that prompted him to bring the best he had as an offering.

Question 8. God will not be pleased with any worship or attempt at being right with him that rests on our efforts or our goodness. God is pleased with faith—the willingness to come to God with empty hands and to receive all that he desires to give in grace. This means that the principle of faith extends beyond just our initial salvation. We are also called to live by faith. Every step in life is made in trust. We depend on God's wisdom and guidance and mercy in every decision and in every moment.

Question 9. We walk in the way of Cain when we come to God filled with pride in ourselves or confidence in our best efforts. We also walk in Cain's way when we reject God's warning or his appeals to repent or change our attitude toward him. A spirit of disregard for the welfare of others is a further mark of the way of Cain.

We walk in Abel's way when we come to God on his terms with hearts that are open to receive from him. Every time we worship or give an offering to God of time or money or effort we have an opportunity to examine our hearts for signs of faith and for an attitude of humility and gratitude to the Lord.

Study 2. Making Difficult Choices: Noah. Hebrews 11:7; Genesis 6:5-22.
Purpose: To demonstrate the importance of faith-filled obedience to God's direction in our lives.
General note. You as the group leader may want to acquaint yourself with the entire story of Noah in Genesis 6–9. The purpose of this study is to focus on Noah's faithful obedience to God, but reading the whole account will give you some background that will help you answer questions that may arise.

Also, it would be good to remember that Christians disagree about the scope and impact of the flood on the earth's surface. Don't allow the discussion to become a debate on the flood itself. Try to keep the group's attention on Noah and his actions in response to God's warning.

Question 1. It's likely that Noah had never seen a flood of any kind. Certainly forty days of rain and an inescapable flood were things that Noah had never experienced. A key part of what God asked Noah to believe is that, if Noah acted in obedient faith to God's command, he and his family would survive the coming catastrophe.

Question 2. God chose Noah out of grace: "Noah found favor [the word means "grace"] in the eyes of the LORD" (Gen 6:8). But Noah responded to God's grace by living blamelessly before God. Noah did not earn God's favor by his good works, but his blameless life was his response to God's grace. Would God choose survivors today based on their righteous works or purely out of his gracious choice?

Question 3. Noah demonstrated his faith in God by building a large, box-like structure to house animals and human beings. The ark did not have to navigate anywhere (like a boat); it just had to float and be relatively stable in the water. A giant ark built far from the sea in an area that may have never flooded before must have been quite a sight!

Question 4. Noah could have claimed that he believed God's warning but he would not have survived if he had not built the ark. God may call us to a task and even promise success, but we are responsible to act on the basis of our faith and do the work of preparation. For example, God may assure us that he will provide a job, but we have to send out the resumés. Trying to do it all ourselves erases God's power; waiting only for God to do everything shows that we don't really believe. Genuine faith always produces works of obedience.

Question 5. A direct encounter with God would certainly provide powerful motivation to obey. But as convincing as that initial voice from God might have been for Noah, the impact of the encounter would have faded over time—especially considering that it could have taken Noah 120 years to build the ark. In Genesis 6:3 God declares, "My Spirit will not contend with man forever, for he is mortal; his days will be a hundred and twenty years." This is likely a reference to the span of time between this proclamation and the coming of the flood (Bruce Waltke, *Genesis: A Commentary* [Grand Rapids: Zondervan, 2001], p. 117).

God waited in patience for people to repent and turn to him, but only eight were delivered (1 Pet 3:20). When the work became difficult or when the skeptics challenged him, Noah had to continue to choose to believe God's promise.

Question 6. Human society had deteriorated in Noah's day to the level of uncontrolled wickedness and violence. Sinful human nature expressed itself without restraint. Jesus said that the world would again reach that level of wicked behavior just before his return (Mt 24:37; Lk 17:26-27).

Question 7. The evil influence of the culture would have been very difficult to counteract, but Noah faced other challenges as well. He did not have a written Bible to use in the instruction of his sons, nor was there a larger community of faith where Noah and his family could find encouragement and support. Noah may have had some traditions that were passed down to him through his godly ancestors, and he had God's warning about the flood, but that's all.

Question 8. Noah saw very little response to his message, but God evaluated Noah on the devotion of his heart and the depth of his faith. In the same way, God calls us to faithfulness to him and to his Word. We tend to judge the effectiveness of a ministry on the basis of outward results. God looks at the motives and attitudes behind our works (Prov 21:2; 1 Tim 6:11-12).

Question 9. Don't allow this question to get the group distracted from the main point of the study. Some members may raise issues that others will think are relatively minor problems. Treat each responder with respect.

Study 3. Believing the Impossible: Abraham and Sarah. Hebrews 11:8-16; Genesis 18:1-15; 21:1-7.

Purpose: To encourage us to trust God and his promises even when a situation seems beyond hope or help.

General note. The entire Abraham narrative stretches from Genesis 12 through Genesis 25. If you have time, it will be helpful for you as a group leader to acquaint yourself with the whole story.

Question 1. Abraham's journey of faith began when God appeared to him in the city of Ur and called him to leave his home and follow God to a new land (Gen 12:1-4). Then, after he reached the promised land of Canaan, Abraham lived as a stranger and foreigner there with no permanent residence (Heb 11:9). His faith was further challenged by Sarah's inability to conceive. Yet in all these situations, over twenty-five years of time, Abraham continued to believe that God would fulfill his promise to give Abraham and Sarah children and that their descendants would possess the land of Canaan.

Question 2. Abraham left a developed cultural center to live as a nomad and foreigner in Canaan. He left his extended family and his network of friends and business associates to follow God to an unknown place. You might want to ask as a follow-up: What might have been produced in Abraham if he had refused to respond obediently to God's call? What will such refusal produce in us?

Question 3. People's responses to this question will probably cover a whole spectrum of decisions. Responding to God's call today might mean leaving the comforts of a progressive society to minister to indigenous people in a remote part of the world. It might mean bypassing a lucrative career to use your skills to help those who have no means to pay you. It might mean attending and serving in an inner-city church or helping to plant a new church instead of enjoying the benefits of a suburban megachurch.

Question 4. Social custom would have required Abraham to treat these strangers with respect and hospitality, but Abraham provided a lavish meal and showed deep honor to these men. Joyce Baldwin writes that "there was more than ordinary politeness, even by eastern standards, in Abraham's eagerness to entertain them" (*The Message of Genesis 12–50*, The Bible Speaks Today [Downers Grove, Ill.: InterVarsity Press, 1986], pp. 69-70). We learn later that two of the men were angels (Gen 19:1) and one was the Lord (Gen 18:13, 16-17), yet they appeared as normal human men who ate Abraham's food, washed their feet and rested beneath the great trees. When one of the men named Abraham's wife and even prophesied about her, any suspicions Abraham had that these men were more than men were most likely confirmed.

Question 5. The biggest obstacle for Abraham and Sarah was their age. At one hundred years old, Abraham was long past the normal age to produce children. Sarah was ninety and all her life had been unable to conceive. They were "as good as dead" when it came to producing babies! They also had to think about what it would take to raise a child at their age and if they would even survive long enough to see that child reach maturity.

Question 6. We may be tempted to give up on a life dream or a call from God or a spiritual desire if it takes too long to become a reality. That's when the story of Abraham and Sarah brings renewed encouragement to us to keep trusting God. It's worth noting, however, that even Abraham and Sarah struggled with God's promise as the years passed (see Gen 16:1-2; 17:17-22; 18:10-14; 21:6-7).

Question 7. Abraham and Sarah not only believed God for one child, but they also looked ahead and believed that God would keep his promises completely. They didn't live long enough to see it all happen, but they embraced the fullness of God's promises by faith. The same can be true in our lives. We may not live to see the work of God come to completion in our children or our friends or our church. What we can do is trust that God will do what he says he will do. We can welcome that fulfillment as if it were already a reality. Hebrews 11:1 says that faith is being "certain of what we do not see."

Question 8. Though Abraham was living in tents and though the land was occupied by others, he trusted that God would be faithful to give Israel the Promised Land as their own one day. In faith, he looked ahead to the time when they would build cities and settle down in the land, with Jerusalem as the center. As N. T. Wright comments, "God promised Abraham the land, and the crowning glory of the land was Jerusalem, where the Temple would be built" (*Hebrews for Everyone* [London: SPCK, 2003], p. 133).

The "city" in verse 10 may also refer to the "heavenly Jerusalem," the city God will establish when he fully redeems heaven and earth. Again, Wright is helpful: "In some ancient Jewish writings roughly contemporary with the New Testament, there were pointers to a deeper reality, to the belief that God had established a 'true' or heavenly Jerusalem, waiting for the day when heaven and earth would be remade" (ibid.).

Question 9. Abraham's real pilgrimage was to grow in his understanding of God and in his trust that God would keep his promises to him. The situations and delays Abraham experienced were designed to form Abraham's character and to forge a heart of fierce loyalty to God.

Abraham's pilgrimage was not just to Canaan but also to a heavenly country. His journey on earth was not the end. He and Sarah longed for an eternal home where they would enjoy unbroken fellowship with God. Their journey of faith here was part of God's preparation for an even greater journey in the future.

Question 10. Christians who live by faith realize (like Abraham and Sarah did) that we are nomads and foreigners on earth. Our longing is for another country and another city where God is. Living each day by faith is preparation for the day when God's promises will all be fulfilled in the reality of heaven. God is not ashamed to be the God of those who see life as a pilgrimage to a much better place.

At the same time, the trials, joys, delays and blessings of this life are used by God to develop Christlike character and fierce loyalty to God in us day by day. We are not just looking toward heaven but also being molded into Christ's image by the experiences of life.

Question 11. God responds to those who follow him in faith—including faith in "a better country"—by declaring his loyalty to us. He is not ashamed to be called "God" by those who trust him deeply. God has prepared a wonderful eternal reward—a heavenly city—for those who follow him in confident faith.

Study 4. Anticipating God's Blessing: Isaac. Hebrews 11:17-20; Genesis 27:1-40.

Purpose: To follow Isaac's model of confident trust in God's faithfulness to fulfill his promises.

Question 2. As the leader, you should read Genesis 22:1-14 as the backdrop for this passage in Hebrews and then retell the story in summary form for the benefit of those in the group.

Isaac was not a young boy when this incident occurred. He was a young man who could easily have overpowered or run away from his one-hundred-plus-year-old father. Instead Isaac submitted to Abraham. But he would certainly have remembered God's provision of a ram that died in his place! Abraham even named the place *Yahweh-yireh* ("the LORD will provide").

Isaac also probably would have learned that the Lord can be trusted to keep his promises even in what may appear to us to be a hopeless situation. These lessons would have equipped Isaac to believe God even when he thought all hope was gone.

Question 3. Esau, the firstborn of Isaac's sons, was favored by his father. Esau was a rugged outdoorsman who enjoyed hunting and living off the land. Jacob, who was born holding on to Esau's heel as if to pull him back from being born first, was favored by his mother. Jacob preferred a more settled life in the tents of his family.

Question 4. Because Isaac favored Esau, he wanted to try to pass his blessing on to him and give him the place of prominence in the extended family. Isaac was either trying to "convince" God to see things his way or trying to place God in a situation where God would have to alter his original prophecy. Isaac thought his blessing held more power than God's will! In the end,

Isaac was forced by the circumstances to bring his own desires in line with God's purpose and intention.

Question 5. Jacob and his mother, Rebekah, were unwilling to trust God's sovereign authority to rule and to overrule in human affairs. God had already told Rebekah before the boys were born that the older son would serve the younger (Gen 25:23), but Rebekah and Jacob thought they needed to help God out. As a result, Jacob lied repeatedly to Isaac and was a willing partner with his mother in deceiving his father. Jacob's deception cost him a very high price, though. He did receive Isaac's blessing but had to flee out of fear of Esau's revenge, and he most likely never saw him mother, Rebekah, again.

Encourage members of the group to be honest and vulnerable about the level of their trust in God. The best way to prompt that kind of openness is to be open yourself as the group leader. Do you try to help God out when things aren't going like you think they should? Have you deceived others at times in order to get something you wanted? Tough questions—but honest self-evaluation is one of the ways we grow in faith!

Question 6. The patriarchal blessings are not to be regarded as messages from the Lord. They simply represented the hopes and wishes of a father for his son. God was not obliged to follow these parental wishes. The father's blessing had great influence, however, in the cultural setting of ancient Canaan and in the way the extended family responded to an heir (John Walton, *Genesis*, The NIV Application Commentary [Grand Rapids: Zondervan, 2001], pp. 554-55).

Therefore, Isaac was trusting in cultural traditions to try to get his way with God. He knew that God had prophesied that the older son would serve the younger son, but he thought he could get around that by bestowing his blessing on Esau, not Jacob. Furthermore, the blessing ceremony required witnesses to confirm its legality, but Isaac was prepared to pass on the blessing to Esau secretly (Joyce Baldwin, *The Message of Genesis 12–50*, The Bible Speaks Today [Downers Grove, Ill.: InterVarsity Press, 1986], p. 114). Isaac was engaged in a deception of his own!

God certainly did not approve of Jacob's deception and lies, but God was not thwarted or hindered by it either. God was not bound to bless Jacob just because Isaac ended up blessing him any more than he would have been bound to bless Esau if Isaac had managed to bless him. God bestows his blessings on those whom he desires to bless.

Jacob's story reveals that (at times) God allows "success" in sin because he has a greater lesson to teach later on. God's timing is perfect. At the right time, later in Jacob's life, God reminded him of this sin through the actions of a trusted family member who deceived Jacob! So the consequences of Jacob's deception came to full fruit in God's time. "The success of sin is short lived" (Walton, *Genesis*, p. 567).

Question 7. Despite evidence of a lack of faith in God's power on Isaac's part, he *did* believe that God would honor his promises to Abraham that were repeated to him and that he repeated to Jacob (Gen 22:15-18; 27:28-29; 28:3-4). He had faith that, through himself and then through Jacob, the descendants of Abraham would become a great people, and that God would bring his blessing upon all mankind through this tiny, seemingly insignificant family.

Question 8. The purpose of this question is to prompt the members of your group to think about the person in their life they seek approval from most. If a person answers that they genuinely seek the Lord's approval most, ask them for a specific example of how they seek God's approval. The question may uncover some painful issues of seeking to please unresponsive parents or spouses. The point is not to try to resolve those issues but to help people name and face them honestly in a safe, nonjudgmental setting.

Question 10. The goal of the study is to place our future into God's hands. That doesn't mean we don't plan and pursue our dreams, but we place those dreams on the altar and willingly offer them to God. We yield our future to God in faith, confident that he will keep his promises to bless us even if it means the sacrifice of our "Isaac"—our dearest relationship or dream. And we refuse to rely on our own resources (and deceptions) to accomplish what we think God desires. Instead we live in obedience to God and trust him to work in the situations of life to accomplish what he desires.

Study 5. Faith for the Future: Jacob. Hebrews 11:20-22; Genesis 48:1-22.
Purpose: To prompt us to be more intentional about building faith in the lives of those closest to us.

Question 1. As the group leader, you might want to read the biblical accounts of Jacob and Joseph to prepare yourself for this study: Genesis 25:19-34; 27–33; 35; 37; 39–47. A simple chart of Abraham's descendants might help to keep the discussion on track.

Each major descendant of Abraham demonstrated his faith by his actions. The father's act of blessing his descendants was an act of faith in God's promises to bless all the descendants of Abraham (Gen 12:2-3; 17:7). Once a father's blessing was pronounced it could not be reversed or rescinded (Gen 27:33-38). The blessing made God's promises specific and tangible; it was a faith-filled anticipation of all that God would do in fulfillment of his promises.

Isaac was deceived into pronouncing the family blessing on Jacob instead of Esau (Gen 27), but Isaac knew that the blessing was binding and would not fail. Later Isaac repeated his blessing on Jacob with full knowledge of what he was doing (Gen 28:1-4). He realized that God had taken what was intended as a deceitful act and had used it to accomplish his sovereign will to bless Jacob and to reject Esau.

Jacob believed God's promises too. As an old man, he blessed Joseph's two sons, crossing his hands and reversing the customary order of the blessing at God's direction. Jacob was confident about the future even though his act was contrary to social convention and tradition. Furthermore, Jacob made Joseph promise that he would not bury him in Egypt but would take his body back to Canaan and bury his bones in the cave Abraham had purchased for the burial of Sarah (Gen 47:28-31). His request to be buried in Canaan was an expression of faith in God's promise to give the people of Israel that land.

Joseph was certain that nothing would thwart God's promise that Israel would someday possess the land of Canaan—so certain that he too requested that his bones (his mummy?) be buried in Canaan, not in Egypt. More than three hundred years later, Moses and the people of Israel brought Joseph's bones out of Egypt (Ex 13:19), and Joshua buried his remains near Shechem after Israel's conquest of the land (Josh 24:32).

Question 2. Expect a wide range of answers to this question. A good follow-up question for each one who responds is, What is the basis of this promise? Is it a biblical promise, or is it drawn from some other source or experience? Also, emphasize how faith in the promise affects the person's life today. Do they live any differently because of their confidence in God's word to them?

Question 3. Jacob reveals several experiences from his past that moved him from a manipulative schemer to a person who confidently trusts in God: (1) God had appeared to Jacob and had repeated the promises that had been given to Abraham and Isaac (Gen 28:10-21), (2) God had given Jacob an abundance of sons (which was already a partial fulfillment of God's promises to him), (3) Rachel's burial in Canaan was a link to the land that God had promised (Gen 35:16-20), and (4) God had exalted Joseph in Egypt and then reunited Jacob and Joseph.

Question 4. By claiming Joseph's two sons as his own, Jacob was raising Ephraim and Manasseh to the same status in Israel as his natural sons and giving Joseph a double portion of his blessing and inheritance, even though Joseph was not the eldest of Jacob's sons. From Jacob's sons came the "tribes" or "clans" (extended families) that made up the people of Israel. There is no tribe of Joseph, however, because Joseph is represented in the two tribes of Ephraim and Manasseh.

Question 5. When Jacob (also called Israel in this passage in Genesis) began his blessing of Joseph's sons, he crossed his hands. This act was contrary to cultural custom. His right hand (and the greater blessing) rested on the younger of Joseph's sons, and his left hand (and the lesser blessing) rested on the older son. It seems ironic that Joseph objected to this reversal since it was his grandfather Isaac's blessing of Jacob (the younger son) that had now brought God's blessing to Joseph and his sons.

Question 6. God was demonstrating to Joseph (and to us) that he is sovereign in his choice to bless or to withhold blessing. God is not governed by human convention or custom or even human will. He is free to work as he desires to accomplish his purposes. Jacob's unorthodox move also demonstrates that God often works in ways we don't expect or can't predict. The proof is all the way through Abraham's line: it was not Abraham's firstborn son, Ishmael, who received the blessing but his younger son, Isaac; it was not Isaac's eldest son, Esau, who was the recipient of God's promises but his younger son, Jacob; the double part of God's blessing did not go to Jacob's first son, Reuben, but to Joseph, a much younger son; and now Joseph's second son, Ephraim, receives the major blessing instead of his eldest son, Manasseh. We can't lock God in to our way of doing things. He's so much more creative than we are. So look for answers to prayer or the blessings of God in ways and through avenues you don't expect!

Question 7. You may have some group members respond to this question with pain or deep longing. Be prepared to offer comfort or support to them. Some may be skeptical of such a pronouncement and might need to be reminded that God may choose to bless them in very unexpected ways.

Question 8. Believing that Joseph and his brothers (or their descendants) will one day return to Canaan and possess it, Jacob gives Joseph a tiny slice of the land that Jacob had conquered as his own. This is a foreshadowing of Israel's future conquest of the entire land—more than three hundred years after Jacob's death. (God had told Abraham that his descendants would be strangers in Egypt for four hundred years [Gen 15:13].)

Question 10. Genuine worship is the acknowledgment of God's worth, the exaltation of God's character and goodness. Jacob's blessing of Joseph's sons and his affirmation of the ultimate fulfillment of God's promises to his family were acts that exalted God's sovereign authority, his unlimited power and his desire to bless purely out of his grace.

Question 11. Try to get the group to focus on the spiritual strengths revealed in this particular study and in the actions of Joseph and Jacob. Then lead people to name some practical ways to impart these strengths to the people they influence.

Now or Later. Jacob calls God his "Angel" (Gen 48:16), not because God *is* an angel (he is not), but because God *acts* toward Jacob as a powerful and protective angel or messenger.

Study 6. Resting on a Trustworthy God: Moses. Hebrews 11:23-29; Exodus 12:21-36.

Purpose: To bring us to the place of enduring confidence in God through a difficult season or an entire lifetime.

Question 1. The entire biblical narrative about Moses encompasses most of the Old Testament books of Exodus, Numbers and Deuteronomy. The key portions for you as a leader to read are Exodus 1–20, Numbers 13–14 and 20, and Deuteronomy 34. Some members of your group may know a lot about Moses; almost everyone will have some fragmentary knowledge of his life. You may want to write the major events on a 120-year timeline or on three successive 40-year timelines to represent the three phases of Moses' life: 40 years in Egypt, 40 in Midian and 40 in the wilderness leading the people of Israel. Don't try to get every event of his life written down, but some perspective on how events unfolded will be helpful. Focus on the fresh insight that comes from the passage in Hebrews.

Question 2. Exodus 1:15–2:10 is useful in answering this question, as it provides some context for Moses' life (like the murder of the male infants). Moses' parents, Amram and Jochebed (Ex 6:20), acted in direct defiance of the king's law but in active obedience to what they knew God would want them to do. The text literally says that Moses was a "beautiful" child (Ex 2:2 NASB). The NIV conveys the fuller meaning: "he was no ordinary child" (Heb 11:23). Perhaps God spoke to Moses' parents and revealed what Moses was to become. Certainly Moses' parents were willing to believe that God had not abandoned his people.

The title "Pharaoh" was what the Egyptians called their ruler. It was not his personal name but his title of authority.

Question 3. Even though Moses was raised in Pharaoh's household and had a title of prominence in Egypt, he made a deliberate choice to turn away from the path of power and influence (his first decision). Moses decided it was better to be mistreated in the company of God's people (his second decision) than to be treated well in the halls of political and economic power. He said no to one path and yes to a more difficult path in choosing to align himself with the Hebrew people.

Question 4. God is not asking all Christians to be monks or missionaries. There may come a time, however, when we have to choose between obedience to God and the next step up in a career. A Christian may have to turn away from a marriage proposal or a business promotion or a lifestyle upgrade in order to obediently follow Christ.

Jesus promised, though, that those who gave up anything for his sake would receive a hundred times as much in spiritual blessings in return (Mk 10:29-30). So, the reward for turning away from a promotion at work might be having more time to disciple your children into ardent followers of Christ. As another example, saying no to a shady financial endeavor may not bring new avenues of wealth, but it will bring the reward of a clear conscience and a pure heart before God.

Question 6. This passage in Hebrews gives us deeper insight into Moses' departure from Egypt than we get in the Exodus passage alone (Ex 2:11-15). Usually this incident of Moses killing the Egyptian guard and fleeing to Midian is viewed as a time of failure in Moses' life (and elements of failure are clearly part of the story); Moses attempted to try to deliver the Israelites his own way (by killing an Egyptian) rather than God's way. But in leaving Egypt after the incident, he was, as Hebrews 11:27 says, acting out of faith in God and not out of fear of the king. Even later when he argued with the Lord at the burning bush about going back to Egypt, Moses seemed to still believe that God would deliver Israel. He was just convinced that God would have to do it through someone else.

Question 7. Certainly we see God's power revealed in this final plague—and his sovereign authority to judge those who resist his will. But we also see God's mercy extended to those in Israel who by faith placed the lamb's blood on the doorposts.

Question 8. Some may see great cruelty in God's actions. Remind them of God's patience with Pharaoh and the Egyptians. God had warned them several times and gradually escalated the severity of the plagues to persuade Pharaoh to let Israel go. God still patiently waits for people to believe in him, but eventually his promises of judgment are fulfilled.

Other members of the group might be strengthened by such demonstrations of God's power—not because people suffer, but because it's a reminder that God will rule and overrule to accomplish what he desires.

Question 9. The need for faith did not end when Moses returned to Egypt as God's deliverer. He had to keep trusting God while the people doubted and Pharaoh resisted. The act of the Passover itself involved great faith on behalf of Moses and the Israelites: faith that God would be true to his promise to spare their children if they obeyed his instructions about putting blood on the doorframes of their homes.

Question 11. This could happen in several ways today. A pastor might instill a congregation to take a new step of faith by encouraging them to trust God's faithfulness. A civic leader might rouse a community or a nation to a new level of action or sacrifice because they believe in his or her character and leadership. A father or family member can change a family's direction by using faith-filled words to challenge them to have confidence in God's direction or God's promises.

Question 12. This question might elicit some very personal or painful answers. Give group members the freedom to share only what they are comfortable with. Try to pray as a group for each situation.

Study 7. Facing Our Fears: Rahab. Hebrews 11:30-31; Joshua 2:1-21.

Purpose: To overcome some of the fears that keep us from fully trusting God.

Introduction. Some later Jewish commentators refer to Rahab as an "innkeeper" rather than a prostitute, but the Hebrew word used in Joshua (*zona*) and the Greek word used in Hebrews (*pornē*) are the normal words for a prostitute (Marten H. Woudstra, *The Book of Joshua*, The New International Commentary on the Old Testament [Grand Rapids: Eerdmans, 1981], p. 69).

Question 1. The story of Joshua's conquest of the city of Jericho and Rahab's deliverance is told in Joshua 1–6. You might want to read the entire account as background for this study. The writer of Hebrews would have assumed that his readers were well acquainted with the biblical narrative.

Question 2. The house of a prostitute offered inexpensive, anonymous lodging in an ancient city. Men would be expected at a house with that reputation. The spies could stay there without being asked a lot of questions. There is no indication that they went to Rahab's house for any immoral purpose. It's even possible that the spies received divine direction to go to her house. God certainly knew that Rahab's heart was open to believe. (See Richard Hess, *Joshua: An Introduction and Commentary*, Tyndale Old Testament Commentaries [Downers Grove, Ill.: InterVarsity Press, 1996], pp. 83-84.)

Question 3. Rahab's lie is the key ethical dilemma of the story, and Christians have divided opinions on whether she was right or wrong in what she did. Some say that the lie was morally wrong; Rahab should have told the truth and trusted God for the results. Other Christians think that a higher moral issue was involved—the protection of God's representatives—and that the lie was justified to thwart the evil planned against them. You will probably find both sides represented in your group!

Question 4. Rahab was seeking protection for herself and her family. She wanted some assurance that her courageous act would be recognized and rewarded. Since the spies owed their lives to her, she wanted her life spared as repayment.

Question 5. Even though Rahab had self-centered motives for her request, the writer of Hebrews saw this as an act of faith because Rahab was convinced that God would give Israel victory over Jericho. She fully believed that God would do what he had promised he would do. Sometimes what appears to be compromised or selfish faith to us is counted by God as an act of complete trust in him.

Question 6. Rahab's faith translated itself into several acts of obedience. First, she hung a piece of scarlet-colored rope from the window of her home (which was part of the wall of Jericho) to mark where she lived, as the spies had instructed her to do. Then Rahab was responsible to gather her family into her home when the siege of Jericho began. Finally, Rahab had to keep the escape of the spies a secret so that they would not be pursued when they left.

Question 7. Rahab's actions showed that her faith was genuine. She had confessed a level of faith to the spies earlier, but her actions here prove that it was more than just words. Her obedience also demonstrated her confidence in the promises of the spies as God's people. She believed that God would give Israel the city and the land. Moreover, Rahab wasn't just seeking a way to escape the coming destruction; she was identifying herself with God's people. Her actions revealed that she believed that Israel's God would extend his grace to a believing Gentile—even a prostitute—and demonstrated her growing personal faith in the Lord God. Joshua 6:25 records Rahab's rescue and her inclusion among the people of Israel from that day forward.

Question 8. Obviously, none of us can force saving faith on a family member or friend. But we can pray for those who have not yet received Christ, and we can be a faithful witness to them. Also, by our word and example, we can encourage those who are believers to grow in grace and in holy living.

Question 10. Faith is the conviction that God can overcome any barrier or resistance or obstacle to reach a person with his grace—and that God can use someone like you or me to be the instrument to open the door. As each person shares their fears, encourage them to trust God with that fear and to act courageously in faith.

Study 8. Your Heroic Faith. Hebrews 11:32–12:3.

Purpose: To challenge us to continue on in our pursuit of a faith-filled life.

Question 1. The first group of faith heroes saw God do miraculous works of power in response to their faith. Up to this point, the writer of Hebrews has focused on the earliest examples of faith in the Old Testament. Now he gives a breathless survey of judges, kings and prophets. He picks one person after another and one event after another that stand out in his mind as models of courageous faith.

Question 2. We usually respond to stories of faith and God's powerful works with joy and awe, with exclamations of "God is so good!" But it's also possible to respond with some resentment, such as "Why doesn't God do something like that for me?" Or our response may be to dismiss the possibility that God would work like that today; we might think to ourselves, *God did some pretty spectacular things in the past, but he seems far away right now.* Allow group members to answer the question freely and without judgment from others.

Question 3. The second group saw their faith "rewarded" with prison or torture or death. Today, these are the faithful believers who rarely speak in public or write a book. God responds to their faith by empowering them to persevere to the end and to trust God even if the end isn't what they desired or asked for.

Question 4. Those who claim that genuine faith always results in victory or deliverance haven't taken into account the millions of believers over the centuries who were persecuted or martyred for their faith. Those who wander in destitute poverty because of their commitment to Jesus are as highly commended by God for their faith as those who have experienced a miraculous deliverance from danger. We cannot judge the reality or depth of a person's faith simply by the outward circumstances of his or her life.

Question 5. Some interpreters see these examples of faith from the past as models for those of us who live today. They left their witness to us in Scripture, and we can learn what it means to trust God by following in their steps. Other interpreters believe these past witnesses are more engaged with us than that, claiming that they not only left a pattern behind but are also cheering us on today. Abel and Abraham and Moses sit in the grandstands of heaven and, by the example of their lives, urge us to press on in faithful endurance. *The Message* reads, "Do you see what this means—all these pioneers who blazed the way, all these veterans cheering us on?" For a discussion of both views, see William Lane, *Hebrews 9–13*, Word Biblical Commentary (Dallas: Word, 1991), p. 407.

Question 6. The author of Hebrews uses the idea of a great audience of witnesses to move to the picture of the Christian life as a race. We are called to strip off whatever weighs us down in our perseverance toward the final goal.

These may be good things in themselves, but they slow us down and pull our attention away from the important things. For example, I may enjoy a hobby or watching sports—not evil things in themselves—but they may keep me from pursuing a deeper relationship with the Lord or discipling my children or taking on a ministry to other believers.

We also put aside whatever sin gets our feet tangled. Instead of stumbling over and over, we make a deliberate choice to put that sin aside. That choice is only the first step though. Putting aside sin also involves yielding ourselves continually to the Holy Spirit's power and making ourselves accountable to other believers who will help us leave the old, entangling habits behind.

That frees us to run with endurance. The Christian life is not a sprint that takes all our effort for a very short time. This spiritual race is a marathon—a route already marked out by Jesus and by the feet of faithful men and women who have gone before. Now we run the same route of faith, and we keep at it. Their example encourages us to remain faithful. The pull of other Christians running the race with us today keeps us going as well. Probably the most essential element in endurance is a firm resolve before the Lord that we will not drop out but will make every effort to cross the finish line well.

Question 7. Successful runners do not look at their feet or at the other runners in the race or even at the crowds cheering in the stands. They focus their attention on the goal. Jesus stands at the goal line of our faith race, ready to receive us and reward us for a race run well. When exhaustion or discouragement or hardship drags us down and makes us tempted to leave the race of faith, looking at the willingness of Jesus to endure the cross for us provides new energy and commitment to keep on.

Question 8. Jesus ran the race set before him even though it included the hatred and insults of wicked people and the agony of the cross. If he took all that for us, we should certainly be able to endure whatever suffering or insults come our way for him.

In addition to endurance and perseverance, Jesus' example demonstrates the kind of dependence on God we will need to complete the race. Other qualities we learn from Jesus are patience to wait for God's timing, wisdom to respond appropriately to attack and slander, forgiveness toward those who oppose us, and concern for people around us who are hurting. To be like Jesus means (among many things) to endure difficult times with the same grace and faithfulness he had.

Question 9. Encourage each group member to be honest about where they are in the race. Maybe you as a leader can set the pace by being transparent

about your own struggles in the life of faith. Try to draw some specific suggestions for each person from these verses in Hebrews 11 and 12. Even if a
person believes they are running steadily, you could suggest some specific
practices that will encourage them to endure and to focus their attention on
Jesus who is standing at the finish line.

Now or Later. As you finish this study, you might want to have a meal together
or even just light refreshments. Ask each person to share which Bible character
they identified most closely with and why. The formal study may come to an
end but the race of faith lasts a lifetime.

*Douglas Connelly (MDiv and MTh, Grace Theological Seminary) is the senior pastor at
Davison Missionary Church, near Flint, Michigan. He is also the author of* Angels Around
Us *(InterVarsity Press) and* The Bible for Blockheads *(Zondervan), as well as seventeen
LifeBuilder Bible Studies.*

Printed in Great Britain
by Amazon